LIVING WITH FOOD ALLERGIES

ABDO
Publishing Company

LIVING WITH FOOD ALLERGIES

by Carol Hand

Content Consultant
Devon Golem, Registered Dietitian,
Rutgers University, New Brunswick, New Jersey

LIVING WITH HEALTH CHALLENGES

CREDITS

Published by ABDO Publishing Company, PO Box 398166, Minneapolis, MN 55439. Copyright © 2012 by Abdo Consulting Group, Inc. International copyrights reserved in all countries. No part of this book may be reproduced in any form without written permission from the publisher. The Essential Library™ is a trademark and logo of ABDO Publishing Company.

Printed in the United States of America,
North Mankato, Minnesota
102011
012012

 THIS BOOK CONTAINS AT LEAST 10% RECYCLED MATERIALS.

Editor: Holly Saari
Copy Editor: Karen Latchana Kenney
Series design and cover production: Becky Daum
Interior production: Kazuko Collins

Library of Congress Cataloging-in-Publication Data
Hand, Carol, 1945-
  Living with food allergies / by Carol Hand.
      p. cm. -- (Living with health challenges)
  Includes bibliographical references.
  ISBN 978-1-61783-128-7
  1. Food allergy--Juvenile literature. I. Title.
  RC596.H35 2012
  616.97'3--dc23
                              2011033156

CONTENTS

EXPERT ADVICE

I have been a registered dietitian since 2003 and have counseled many individuals with food allergies. Most of my clients have been diagnosed by age 18, which is typical, because food allergies usually develop early in life. In general, adolescents begin taking more responsibility for their diets. Dietary decisions are often complex, though, and can be further complicated when a food allergy is added to a person's life. This is why it is so important for individuals with food allergies to seek the help of qualified professionals, such as physicians and registered dietitians.

It's important to remember that most individuals with food allergies live healthy lives. You are not alone—many sources of information are available, whether they are found in your community or on the Internet. My few key pieces of advice for you are:

Know what you consume. By the time you have been diagnosed, you are very aware of the specific ingredient that causes your body to react. Now, you must go beyond the basics. Always read product labels, talk with servers or chefs when eating out, and communicate with your pharmacist if you are taking medication. Take the extra step to know what you are putting on and in your body.

Be prepared. Listen to your body and know the signs and symptoms of its reactions to an allergen. Always carry your medication. Have a plan of action in the case of accidental consumption. Carry appropriate snacks with you at all times. Also, tell your friends and teachers about your allergy.

Focus on foods you can consume. Eliminating certain foods from your diet can reduce the intake of important nutrients your body needs, so it is important to find other sources of these nutrients. It is possible to have a varied and well-rounded diet even when eliminating an allergen. Make a long list of foods that do not contain your allergen. Consult with a registered dietitian to find replacement foods that will give you adequate nutrition. Communicate with others who have the same food allergy to find more ways to enjoy the foods you can eat.

Get support. Many of my clients who were diagnosed with food allergies find that communicating with others with the same food allergy enriched their lives. They are able to discuss not only their diets but also similar situations they went through and feelings and thoughts they had. Joining a local or online group can lead to peace of mind.

Remember, your food allergy is something that can be managed. Doing so will allow you to lead a balanced and healthy life.

—Devon Golem, Registered Dietitian, Rutgers University, New Brunswick, New Jersey

HOW CAN I BE ALLERGIC TO FOOD?

Lin is sitting in the library trying not to groan in pain. Her stomach cramps are getting worse, and she feels like she might throw up. Finally, she can't stand it anymore. She gets permission to go to the bathroom and rushes out of the room. After a severe bout of

The discomfort and pain an undiagnosed food allergy brings can make it hard for you to focus in school.

diarrhea, she feels better, although she's still a little nauseated. I should have known better, she thinks.

Lin knows she gets sick like this every time she eats ice cream or drinks milk. But today, she couldn't resist eating a scoop of chocolate ice cream at lunch.

Lin is sure she must have a milk allergy. She knows about allergies because her best friend, Erica, has had a peanut allergy since she was very young. If anything that contains peanuts even touches Erica's mouth, her lips begin to tingle, and she begins gasping for air because her throat closes up almost immediately. It's really scary. Erica must be very careful not to eat anything containing peanuts—ever. She even carries an injection of epinephrine, a hormone she must give herself if she accidentally eats something with peanuts. Otherwise, Erica could die.

Lin thinks she must have an allergy, too. *That must be why dairy products make me sick*, she thinks. But why are her symptoms so different, and so much less dangerous, than Erica's? Maybe she just has a milder allergy. Lin's parents tell her it's just an intolerance and not to worry about it. "Just stay away from milk and ice cream, and you'll be fine," her mother assures her.

FOOD ALLERGY OR FOOD INTOLERANCE?

No wonder Lin is confused. It's logical to think that because she and her friend both have bad reactions to foods, they must both have food allergies. But actually, there are many reasons why people react negatively to food, and only a small percentage of those reactions are allergic reactions. Most of the reactions, like Lin's, are food intolerances.

A food allergy occurs when your immune system attacks a particular food that you have eaten. Normally, the immune system protects you from dangerous invaders, such as disease-causing bacteria and viruses. But when you have a food allergy, your immune system mistakenly identifies an ordinary, nutritious food—such

FOOD ALLERGIES BY THE NUMBERS

- Approximately 3.7 percent of adults and 5 to 6 percent of children have food allergies.[1] Other reactions are usually food intolerances.
- In the United States, food allergies affect approximately 12 million people, including 3 million children.[2]
- The highest incidence of food allergies is in children under age three—every 1 in 17 children; the incidence in the total population is approximately 1 in 25.[3]

as peanuts—as an invader and produces antibodies to act against the food. Antibodies are protein molecules that are made to destroy antigens, which are other proteins found on or in the invader—in this case, the food. An antigen that causes an allergic reaction is called an allergen. Allergens trigger the release of chemicals that cause typical allergy symptoms: stuffy nose, watery eyes, skin rashes, and more. Severe allergic reactions include anaphylaxis, a life-threatening allergic condition.

ANAPHYLAXIS EXPLAINED

Anaphylaxis is a severe allergic reaction that includes constriction of airways, trouble breathing, dizziness, weak or fast pulse, rash, and vomiting. The reaction can occur within a few seconds or more than a half hour after exposure to an allergen. Common foods that cause anaphylaxis include peanuts, fish, milk, and eggs. Anaphylaxis should be treated immediately with epinephrine, which is a hormone that increases the circulation of blood in order to reverse the allergic response. Epinephrine can be injected into the thigh with an autoinjector, which is a syringe and needle combination. If you might be prone to anaphylaxis, it's recommended to carry an epinephrine autoinjector with you at all times. If not treated, anaphylaxis can lead to unconsciousness and death.

Unlike allergies, a food intolerance does not trigger immune system responses. Often, food intolerance results from the body's

When you have a food allergy, foods that should be okay to eat become off limits.

inability to make a necessary chemical. Lin, for example, has lactose intolerance. Lactose is the sugar found in milk products. Lin's body cannot make the enzyme lactase, which breaks down lactose. So, when she drinks milk or eats ice cream, it remains in her system and causes bloating, pain, and stomach cramps. As soon as the undigested milk is removed from her system, she is fine again.

Some cheeses and sauerkraut contain irritating chemicals that can cause allergy-like symptoms without stimulating antibody production. Compounds in bananas and avocados can trigger migraines. These are examples of food intolerances, not food allergies, because the immune system does not produce antibodies that act against the food.

When you have a true food allergy, even a tiny amount of the food can trigger an allergic reaction, and it happens every time you eat the food. With a food intolerance, you may be able to eat small portions of the food with little or no effect, but suffer from a reaction when you overdo it. Knowing the difference between allergy and intolerance is not enough to diagnose yourself. If you think you may have a food allergy or intolerance, see a doctor for a diagnosis. He or she must perform special tests to distinguish between the two.

FOOD ALLERGIES AND OTHER ALLERGIES

Food allergies are more similar to other types of allergies— such as allergies to mold, pollen, or bee stings—than to food intolerances. All allergies are caused in the same way:

TELLTALE SIGNS

Non-life-threatening food allergy symptoms include:

- Nasal congestion
- Runny nose
- Itchy mouth, skin, or ear canal
- Swelling of lips or skin
- Nausea or vomiting
- Abdominal pain and/ or diarrhea
- Flushed skin
- Hives or eczema
- Red, itchy eyes

Food allergies and food intolerances are sometimes confused. You'll need to go to the doctor to figure out which one you have.

your immune system overreacts to something in your environment. Additionally, all allergens trigger the same cascade of responses in the immune system and lead to many of the same symptoms.

Some people have only one kind of allergy, while others have a combination. For example, if you have a pollen allergy, eating cucumbers or watermelon may also trigger symptoms because they contain proteins that are similar to pollen proteins. Sometimes people have minor allergy symptoms—they may sneeze throughout pollen season but are otherwise healthy. Others have severe symptoms that impair their health and require constant treatment.

TELLTALE SIGNS II

Life-threatening symptoms of a food allergy include problems with breathing or circulation, which can lead to anaphylaxis. These symptoms include:

- Throat tightness
- Wheezing
- Shortness of breath or trouble breathing
- Turning blue (indicates lack of oxygen)
- Tongue swelling and trouble swallowing
- Fainting or turning pale (indicates blood pressure drop)
- Chest pain
- Dizziness or light-headedness
- Weak pulse

NOW WHAT?

If you suspect you have a food allergy, the first step is to get tested and find out for sure—so it's off to the doctor! If you are diagnosed with a food allergy, you'll need to alter some eating behaviors, but your life won't change drastically. You'll probably become a nutrition expert because you must learn to take charge of your diet. And you'll become more responsible for

You'll need to see a doctor who can test you for a food allergy. If you have one, you've taken the first step to feeling better.

your health. It could lead to positive changes in your life, making you feel even better! When you're in doubt or feeling overwhelmed, help is available. A good way to learn to live with a food allergy is to read more about it. In this book, you'll find out how allergies change your body. You'll also learn how to respond to those changes so you can still live your life without being confined by your allergy.

ASK YOURSELF THIS

- *After reading the difference between a food allergy and a food intolerance, which one do you think you have? Why?*

- *How can you determine exactly which foods trigger your symptoms?*

- *Are you worried that having a food allergy will change your life drastically? Why? Who can you talk to about your questions and concerns?*

- *What lifestyle changes might you have to make if you have a food allergy? How do you think it might be difficult to make these changes?*

WHY ME? CAUSES

Jason looks around the restaurant and thinks, *This will be a night to remember!* It's prom and Jason is thrilled that Gina agreed to go with him. She's laughing and chatting with their friends as the group waits for the meal. When the shrimp cocktail appetizer arrives, they

The onset of a food allergy can happen at any time, during a regular night at home for dinner or during a special occasion.

all pause to admire the presentation and then grin at each other. "Let's dig in!" says Jason, and he takes his first-ever bite of shrimp.

As he chews, Jason notices his lips and tongue start to tingle and his face feels itchy. Jason touches his cheek. It feels bumpy and hot. He begins coughing and feels the need to clear his throat. He starts to speak and gasps instead. His throat feels tight and he can't get any air. He starts to panic. "I can't breathe," he gasps. His friends are shocked, but one grabs her cell phone and calls 9-1-1. Minutes later, an ambulance arrives and emergency medical technicians are at Jason's side.

"He can't breathe. We don't know what happened. He ate shrimp, and then he couldn't breathe," Gina says.

"He is having a severe allergic reaction," says the technician, as he sticks a pen-like device into Jason's leg. "He should be okay."

But Jason still goes to the emergency room afterward, just in case. He's lucky to have great friends—they came with him to the hospital. After about an hour, he is released, and they eventually make it to the prom. It is definitely a night to remember—just not quite the memories they were expecting!

An unexpected food allergy reaction can be very scary and could result in a trip to the emergency room.

THE ALLERGIC RESPONSE

Jason was just trying a new food at a restaurant when he was catapulted into the world of food allergies. As Jason's experience shows, not all allergies appear at birth. Some, including shellfish allergies, can develop unexpectedly when you're a teenager or even an adult. What exactly happens when you have an allergic response?

It might help to think of it this way: Have you ever met a person who, for no reason you can quite pinpoint, just rubs you the wrong way? The person bothers you, even though other people seem to like him or her. This is similar to what happens when cells in your immune system "meet" a food you're allergic to. The allergen irritates your white blood cells, which are part of your immune system, and the white blood cells respond by making special antibodies to act against that allergen. Antibodies are also called immunoglobulins (Igs). The kind that triggers allergies is called immunoglobulin E (IgE). Production of IgEs occurs the first time you come into contact with an allergen, which sensitizes you to that allergen. Thereafter, your cells remember the allergen, and you will have an allergic reaction every time you encounter it.

Let's look at how this works. Suppose you are allergic to eggs, and you accidentally eat something that contains eggs. The egg allergen causes

FOOD ALLERGIES STATISTICS

- Approximately 10 percent of children with severe cow's milk allergy are also allergic to beef.[1] Some children will also react to sheep's or goat's milk.
- Approximately 20 percent of children with wheat allergies also have an allergy to rye or barley.[2] Oat and rice proteins generally do not cause allergies.

Your mouth is often one of the first body parts affected when you've encountered an allergen.

an instant alert to IgEs embedded on the outside of mast cells. The antibodies were made the first time you encountered the egg allergen, so they are able to recognize and attach to it. When the allergen and the antibodies attach, the mast cells release their chemicals as a protective mechanism. The chemicals, which include histamines, are released to promote inflammation, which is necessary to fight harmful substances and promote healing. White blood cells called basophils also release histamines. Your mouth and lips feel warm and begin to itch and swell. Within minutes your whole mouth is hot and painful. This rapid series of reactions is called the allergic inflammatory response.

The skin is also affected by allergies. Skin symptoms tend to be uncomfortable but minor; they include inflammation and hives, an itchy red rash. Then, the digestive system is affected. The mouth may itch, tingle, or have a metallic taste. Shortly after, the person may suffer from stomachache, nausea, cramps, vomiting, or diarrhea. Severe reactions begin with respiratory symptoms. Any trouble swallowing or breathing may signal an asthma attack. The circulatory system is affected by a rapid drop in blood pressure, which causes dizziness. This signals the onset of anaphylaxis.

Often, when your body responds to a genuine illness-causing threat, such as bacterium viruses, you are not even aware of it. Specific antibodies are triggered to attack and dispose of the invader, but the antibodies are not IgE antibodies, so there is no allergic inflammatory response. When you encounter an allergen, however, your IgE antibodies overreact, causing a rapid, full-scale immune reaction against the allergen, which it should consider typically harmless.

MAJOR FOODS THAT CAUSE ALLERGIES

Any food can cause an allergy, but 90 percent of all food allergies are caused by only eight foods: cow's milk, eggs, peanuts, tree nuts, fish, shellfish, wheat, and soy.[3] Allergies can change with age. Children are most often allergic to eggs, milk, peanuts, and fruits, especially tomatoes and strawberries. Most young people outgrow nut allergies by age six and eggs and milk allergies by age 16, but after this, allergies are outgrown much more slowly.[4] The most common allergies in adults are shellfish, tree nuts, peanuts, eggs, and fish.

With all food allergies, your body reacts negatively to a specific protein allergen in the offending food. The type of protein is different in each food. For example, the protein is albumin in egg white, casein in milk, and lectin in peanuts.

Allergies to peanuts and seafood

IMMUNOGLOBULINS

Five kinds of Igs help fight infection. Only one type participates in allergic reactions.

IgA: Protects mucous membranes from foreign invaders

IgD: Full function still unknown, but acts as a receptor for antigens

IgE: Fights parasites and is involved in allergic reactions to pollen and food

IgG: Most common antibody; facilitates the destruction of foreign substances

IgM: First antibodies produced to fight infection

tend to last throughout a person's life, and both can be very severe. Peanuts are legumes and are related to beans, peas, and soy. Many people with peanut allergies are also allergic to common tree nuts, such as pecans and walnuts. Peanut allergies tend to show up in early childhood. Up to 20 percent of reactions to peanuts and tree nuts result in anaphylaxis.[5] Fifty to 62 percent of people who die from food-related anaphylaxis every year ingested peanuts and another 15 to 30 percent ingested tree nuts.[6]

Approximately half the people with one type of seafood allergy have other types of fish allergies as well.[7] In the United States, approximately 30,000 people are brought to emergency rooms each year suffering from anaphylaxis caused by reactions to seafood, and approximately 200 die.[10]

Finally, if you don't have an allergy to one of the eight main foods, it doesn't mean you

SESAME ALLERGIES ON THE RISE

Sesame allergies are increasing rapidly in the United States. The reason may be the increased ethnic diversity of diets. The more a food is consumed, the more it is reported as an allergen. The likely reason sesame allergies are increasing is due to the increased availability and consumption of sesame seeds and other sesame products. Seventy percent of people with sesame allergies are also allergic to tree nuts and 65 percent to peanuts.[8] Children with tree nut allergies are three times more likely to have a sesame allergy.[9]

COMMON FOOD ALLERGIES

Type of Allergy	% of People Affected	% Who Outgrow and Age Outgrown	Usual Severity of Reactions*
Egg	1.5–3.2% of children	68% by age 16	Usually mild
Fish/ Shellfish	2.3% of total population	Only 2–5% of children; 60% have first reaction as an adult	Often severe
Milk	2.5% of children under 3	19% by age 4; 80% by age 16	Varies
Peanut	1.2% of children	20% by age 6	Often severe
Soy	0.5% of children	Most by age 3	Usually mild
Tree Nut	1.2% of total population	9% by age 6	Often severe
Wheat	0.4% of children	Most by age 5; uncommon in adolescents and adults	Varies

*These severities are typical of reactions to this allergen, but *any* allergen can cause anaphylaxis.

Data compiled by The Food Allergy & Anaphylaxis Network (FAAN) and American Academy of Allergy Asthma & Immunology

can't have a food allergy. Other food allergies are less common, but they do exist. Proteins in fruits, vegetables, spices, and meats, as well as natural food additives such as dyes and preservatives, may trigger allergies.

ASK YOURSELF THIS

- *What food are you allergic to? What kind of reactions have you had? Have you ever had an emergency? If so, what happened?*

- *How can you tell when you are having an allergic reaction to food and when your immune system is reacting normally?*

- *What symptoms do you have that signal you are having an allergic reaction?*

- *Are you able to tell quickly when your symptoms are becoming serious? How?*

- *Have you outgrown any childhood allergies? Is it likely you will outgrow your present allergies? Why or why not?*

JUST ONE BITE: RISK FACTORS AND COMPLICATIONS

armen and her friend Faiza are sitting in Faiza's kitchen, chatting about their school day. Without thinking, Carmen grabs a peanut butter cookie from the plate on the table and takes a bite. She hasn't even swallowed yet when her mouth and hands start

As Carmen found out, once you have a food allergy you can no longer eat on autopilot. You always need to check the food you're about to eat.

to itch and her lips and throat begin to swell. Within minutes, she begins to wheeze.

Faiza knows about Carmen's peanut allergy, and when she sees Carmen's reaction to the cookie, she dives for Carmen's backpack. She dumps everything out, but she can't find the EpiPen. Carmen has forgotten to bring it. "Call my mom. Tell her to bring one," Carmen gasps.

Fortunately, Carmen's house is nearby. Her mother rushes over and gives Carmen an epinephrine injection just in time. Carmen was beginning to turn blue. After a few seconds, her breathing returns to normal, but she still feels weak. Her mother drives her to the emergency room, just to be safe.

Carmen was lucky this time because her mom was home. But what if she wasn't? Carmen didn't even want to think about it. In the passenger seat on the way back from the hospital, she vowed to always have her EpiPen with her from there on.

WHAT ARE RISK FACTORS?

Risk factors are conditions that increase your likelihood of developing a food allergy or of having a reaction after you develop one. Most risk factors of developing an allergy are beyond your control. However, you can usually control the risk factors of having a reaction. Carmen was careless about both. First, you must always be vigilant about what you eat—you *cannot* forget to check the contents of a food before you eat it. Second, you must *always* keep your medication with you. If Carmen's EpiPen—her brand of epinephrine injection—had been more than a few minutes away, she could have died. Not all allergic reactions are potentially deadly; in fact most of them aren't. So it's easy to become careless. But it's vital to your health and your life to recognize the medical complications that can arise when you have a food allergy and to always be prepared for them.

RISK FACTORS FOR DEVELOPING A FOOD ALLERGY

A parent might say that allergies "run in the family," and this is true to a certain extent. If other family members have asthma, hives, or hay fever, your risk of developing allergies is greater than the risk of your friend whose family members do not have allergies. The likelihood of having an allergy increases up to 50 percent if one parent has an allergy and increases up to 80 percent if both parents have an allergy.[1] But you will not necessarily have the same allergies as your parents. One parent may have

If one of your parents has any kind of allergy, you are more likely to develop a food allergy.

hay fever and the other asthma, while you have allergies to peanuts and strawberries. In other words, allergic tendencies, but not the allergies themselves, can be genetically inherited.

You are more likely to develop a food allergy now if you have had one in the past. If you were allergic to cow's milk as a baby, you might later develop other food allergies. Also, if you have other allergies now, such as reactions to mold or pollen, you are more likely to develop food allergies. Because all allergens trigger the inflammatory response in your body, your genetic tendency toward allergies puts you at risk for whatever allergens you encounter.

Age is also a risk factor. Young children have the most allergies, but many outgrow them as they get older. A new study shows that race and gender are also important. It found that food allergies are higher in children, African Americans, and males. African-American male children were more than four times more likely to have food allergies than the average risk rate.[2]

RISK FACTORS FOR A REACTION

One of the greatest risk factors associated with food allergies is being a teenager. This is because teens sometimes engage in risky behaviors, such as ignoring their allergies or pushing them to the limit. For example, you might think, *Just one little bite can't hurt* or *I haven't had an attack in months. I'll be fine.* Sometimes, as in Carmen's case, a teenager might be forgetful or careless. But more than half of teens in one survey admitted to purposely eating foods they knew they were allergic to, and only 61 percent said they always carried their epinephrine autoinjector with them.[3]

Eating the food you're allergic to and not carrying your medicine are the two riskiest behaviors that can easily be stopped.

Often, risky behaviors occur because teens want to fit in and feel normal. You might feel embarrassed about having to explain your allergies to a waiter or disappointed at having to turn down a treat your friends are enjoying. But before you take a risk, consider the alternatives. How much more embarrassing would it be to break out in hives in front of your friends? What will you do if you have a life-threatening attack and your medication isn't handy? Taking your allergies seriously is a serious matter. Although food allergy deaths are rare, many victims are teens and young adults and, often, they were eating away from home when the allergen was consumed.

RISKY BEHAVIORS TO AVOID

- Taking "just one little bite" of a food you're allergic to
- Failing to carry your allergy medication at all times
- Not telling your friends, teachers, and food workers about your food allergy
- Trying a new food away from home or without medication on hand
- Not getting help immediately when you have a reaction

FOOD ALLERGY COMPLICATIONS

Major complications can occur in someone with food allergies, and they primarily include asthma attacks and anaphylaxis. A severe reaction begins within minutes to more than a half hour after consuming the food and is always signaled by respiratory problems. You may have some initial symptoms of an allergy such as red skin, rash, rapid pulse, swelling, and sweating.

You may also begin to cough or wheeze and feel shortness of breath, indicating that your airway is closing up and you are having an asthma attack. Food allergies are linked to asthma in general, as well. Young children who have egg or cow's milk allergies are more likely to have asthma later in life. Peanut and shrimp allergies are also associated with asthma. People with asthma and food allergies are almost seven times more likely to experience a severe asthma attack than people who have asthma but no food allergies.[4]

Asthma can progress quickly into anaphylaxis if the circulatory system becomes involved. In anaphylaxis, your blood vessels dilate, making your blood pressure decrease rapidly. You will feel dizzy or faint. Any symptom of either respiratory or circulatory distress should alert you to use medication immediately. Because the symptoms appear so quickly and are so intense, it is vital to carry medication

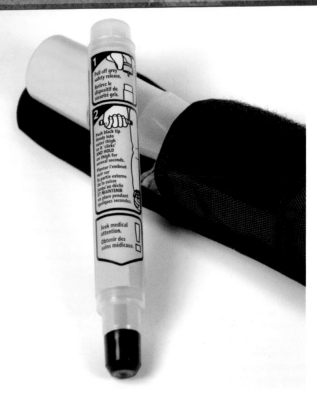

To use an epinephrine autoinjector, take off the cap and stick the needle into your leg. The medicine will enter your body automatically.

(usually in the form of an epinephrine autoinjector) with you at all times.

Eczema, a persistent dry, itchy rash, is most common in young children. It can have many causes, including food allergies, but it is difficult to demonstrate that a food is actually causing the rash. If a food is the cause, it will most likely be a food that is eaten every day. The foods most commonly associated with eczema are eggs, milk, peanuts, soy, and wheat.

CROSS-REACTIVITY

If you are allergic to one substance, you may also be allergic to others having similar proteins. This is called cross-reactivity. A common example of cross-reactivity is oral allergy syndrome, which occurs when people allergic to pollen have cross-reactions with fruits or vegetables having proteins similar to the pollen proteins. For example, if you are allergic to ragweed pollen, you may also react to melons and carrots. The reaction is usually restricted to swelling and severe itching around the mouth and lips. The food allergy tends to begin in late childhood and symptoms are strongest during pollen season. Because cooking destroys the proteins, cooked food is usually safe. Additionally, people with soy allergies sometimes react to related foods, such as peanuts, other legumes, and wheat.

ALLERGIES ON THE RISE

Recently, many types of allergies have been increasing. Food allergies in children increased 18 percent and the rate of peanut allergies doubled between 1997 and 2002.[5] One possible explanation for the

THE DEADLY PEANUT

A highly allergic person can react to the amount of allergen contained in 1/44,000 of a peanut kernel.[6]

rise in allergies is the hygiene hypothesis. This is the idea that most Western societies' excessive cleanliness severely limits the immune system's exposure to harmful organisms. The reduction of harmful substances in the environment reduces the amount of training an immune system receives. So, when food proteins that have a similar shape to harmful substances are present, the immune system will designate the food proteins as harmful. As the immune system has no truly harmful substances to compare the food proteins with, the immune system will begin to attack them.

Thus, the more germs you are exposed to as a child, the less likely you are to develop allergies. It sounds unlikely, but there is considerable evidence for this hypothesis. For example, people in developed countries such as

CROSS-REACTIVITY CULPRITS

Pollens and certain foods may show cross-reactivity. Watch out for these combinations:

- People who are allergic to birch pollen may also be allergic to apple, carrot, celery, cherry, peach, hazelnut, raw potato, or wheat.
- People who are allergic to ragweed pollen may also be allergic to melon, honey, or banana.
- People who are allergic to mugwort pollen may also be allergic to celery, carrot, certain spices, peanuts, kiwi, or apple.
- People who are allergic to grass pollen may also be allergic to melon, tomato, watermelon, orange, or wheat.

The hygiene hypothesis states the fewer germs a child is exposed to, the more limited the immune system can become.

the United States and the United Kingdom have more allergies, and the prevalence of allergies increases with a country's level of development. This could be due to a cleanliness factor or a higher rate of diagnosis. Also, people who attended day care or preschool, have older siblings, or grew up with pets in the house or on farms usually have fewer allergies than those who did not.

ASK YOURSELF THIS

- *Did you have any risk factors for developing a food allergy? What were they?*

- *Do you have any risk factors for having an allergic reaction? What are they? How can you decrease your risk?*

- *In what life situations are you likely to be at risk for an allergic reaction?*

- *What can you do to make sure you are in control of your allergies?*

- *What steps would you follow if you or a friend had an unexpected allergic reaction?*

DO I HAVE ONE? TESTING AND DIAGNOSIS

As a baby, Jessie had a milk allergy, but she outgrew it and has had no food problems since age three. One day recently, though, when she had a glass of milk and a chocolate chip cookie after school, she developed a rash around her mouth, her eyes

Going to the doctor and getting tests done is the only way you can know for sure that you have a food allergy.

began to water, and she had stomach cramps. Her mother was worried Jessie's milk allergy had returned. But the same symptoms occurred several more times when she wasn't drinking milk, although they always occurred during or after meals.

Jessie's mother wants to take her to the doctor, but Jessie has always been nervous about the doctor's office. She hates having the doctor poke and prod her, but this time, it's worse. She's worried about the diagnosis. What if the doctor tells her she does have a food allergy? Does that mean she has to give up foods she likes? Will she be sick for the rest of her life? What will she tell her friends? Can she even go out with her friends anymore? If she does have a food allergy, maybe it's better not to know!

Her mother finally persuades her to go to the doctor. Together, they prepare for the visit. They make a list of Jessie's symptoms and try to remember the foods she ate just before her reactions. Her mother looks up information

"Kids with a food allergy are two to four times more likely to have conditions such as asthma and other allergies."[1]

—*A. M. Branum and S. L. Lukacs, National Center for Health Statistics, 2008* about Jessie's previous milk allergy. They try to think of other things that may have caused the reactions. When they arrive at the doctor's office, the doctor welcomes Jessie and puts her at ease by chatting about school and friends. Jessie takes a deep breath. She still feels nervous, but she's prepared and feels able to handle the diagnosis, whatever it is, with the support of her parents and doctor.

GOING TO THE DOCTOR

It's not easy to determine exactly what foods you are allergic to, but to find out for sure, you must see a doctor. A visit to the doctor can be a bit scary and even embarrassing. But your health and well-being are important, so you need to be honest and open with the doctor. Remember, doctors don't want to make you feel uncomfortable by examining you. They are only looking to find clues to what's making you sick so they can figure out how to make you better. You may begin by visiting your family doctor, who may in turn refer you to an allergy specialist. After your visit, the end result

"I'm not saying that being diagnosed with a food allergy is cause to celebrate, but diagnosis is the first step to relief."[2]

—Robert A. Wood, MD, Chief of Pediatric Allergy and Immunology, Johns Hopkins University School of Medicine, 2007

Think of going to the doctor as the first step in feeling better.

is a diagnosis of your allergies and a treatment plan. Your first allergy visit will probably include two parts: a detailed medical history and a physical exam.

It's a good idea to prepare for the medical history interview by bringing important information with you. You'll find that, like

PREPARING FOR YOUR APPOINTMENT

Before your appointment, complete the following steps:

1. Make a list of your symptoms, suspected foods, and the time a reaction occurred.
2. List other family members who have allergies and their types of allergies.
3. List personal changes or life stresses that might relate to your symptoms.
4. List the medications, vitamins, and supplements you are currently taking.
5. List questions you want to ask the doctor.
6. Gather records of visits to other doctors relating to your allergy symptoms.

Jessie, advance preparation will help you understand your diagnosis and be able to handle whatever changes it might bring. It will also help the doctor learn all he or she needs. The doctor will want to know your current and past symptoms, the foods you think caused them, and the timing and severity of your symptoms. You will probably be asked if there is a family history of allergies and other things going on in your life. These questions will help rule out other possible causes and help determine which foods trigger your symptoms.

The physical exam will provide an overview of your general health and identify or rule out other medical problems. The doctor will probably check your height, weight, pulse, blood pressure, and heartbeat. A nurse might also draw a blood sample, so be prepared for a brief needle stick.

THE ALLERGY TESTS

Various tests are used to determine exactly which food or foods cause you to react. You probably won't have to do all of these tests, but sometimes a combination of tests is needed to make an accurate diagnosis. The following tests are ones you may be given during your doctor's visit or asked to perform after your visit.

Food diary: Your doctor may ask you to keep a diary of everything you eat for a week or two. By listing every food item you eat and how it's prepared along with your symptoms and when they occur, you can help narrow down which foods cause problems. A food diary helps the doctor rule out or suspect specific allergens,

QUESTIONS TO ASK YOUR DOCTOR

Here are some questions you might ask on your first visit:
1. What kinds of tests will you do to diagnose my food allergy? How safe are they?
2. How should I prepare for my allergy tests?
3. How long will the tests take and how soon will I have the results?
4. What can I do to improve my condition while I'm waiting for results?
5. Will I outgrow my food allergies?
6. Will I have to avoid these foods for the rest of my life?
7. What are the usual types of treatments or medications for food allergies?

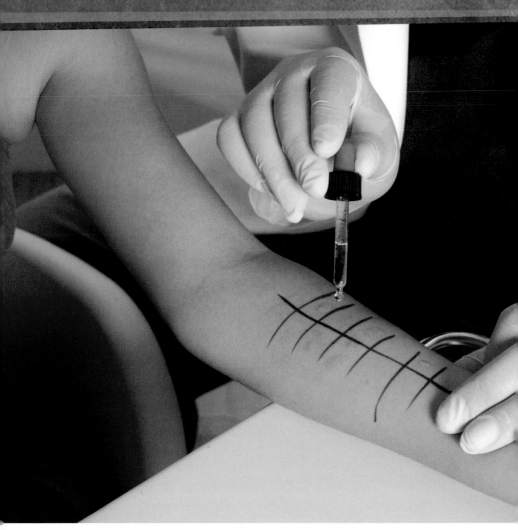

A skin prick test is the most common allergy test.

but it alone is not sufficient to diagnose food allergies.

Skin prick test: The doctor uses a needle that has a small amount of the suspect food allergen on the end and pricks your skin, allowing a tiny amount of the allergen to penetrate under the skin. If you are allergic to the food, a welt will form. The test is inexpensive and can be done in the doctor's office.

Serum IgE test: Blood is drawn and sent to a laboratory to be tested for levels of IgE antibodies to certain foods. A high level of the antibody indicates the presence of an allergy. It is more expensive and takes longer than a skin prick test.

Food elimination: When a particular food is suspected of causing an allergy, the doctor may ask you to completely eliminate it from your diet for seven to 14 days. If allergy symptoms disappear or decrease, this strongly indicates that the eliminated food is causing your allergy.

Food challenge: A suspected allergenic food is given to a patient under a doctor's supervision. If symptoms appear, this confirms that the suspected food is the culprit. A food challenge is done when your health is otherwise stable and you are not taking medications that would interfere with observing symptoms. If you begin to show

SERUM IGE TESTS

A serum IgE test measures the concentration of IgE antibodies dissolved in serum, which is the liquid portion of blood. It may be used instead of a skin prick test for patients with severe skin conditions or a history of anaphylaxis. You may hear the test described as a "RAST," which stands for radioallergosorbent test. This term applies to an outdated form of the test that used radiation.

symptoms, the doctor will discontinue the test and give you medication.

THE DIAGNOSIS

The results of any of these tests combined with your history will often confirm to the doctor's satisfaction the exact food or foods to which you are allergic. For example, a skin prick or serum antibody test with a very strong reaction may be convincing enough. But usually, a second test—perhaps a food elimination followed by a food challenge—will be used to confirm the diagnosis. After your diagnosis, what do you do? Finding a treatment plan for your food allergy is next.

TYPES OF FOOD CHALLENGES

Food challenges are used either to confirm a patient's food allergy diagnosis or to provide an objective test in a research study. Food challenges can be conducted in three ways:

- Open: both patient and observer know the food being tested
- Single-blind: patient is unaware what food is being tested but observer knows
- Double-blind: both patient and observer are unaware of what food is being tested

Open tests are most subjective because the patient's mental or emotional influence can affect the reaction to the food. In double-blind challenges, the food is given in capsule form so neither the patient or observer expects a certain reaction. This makes this food challenge the most objective of the three types.

ASK YOURSELF THIS

- *How much do you know about your own symptoms and your family's history of allergies? How can you learn more?*

- *Have you ever kept a food diary? How would it help you better understand your allergy?*

- *Do you fear going to the doctor? Why? What can you do to overcome your fears?*

- *Do you understand the tests you might have to take? What questions do you have about them to ask your doctor?*

- *What questions about your condition or about allergies in general do you have for the doctor?*

5

EATING THE RIGHT FOODS: TREATMENT

E rnesto has had food allergies for years and complains a lot about his restricted diet. His mom is a great cook, so eating at home isn't a problem. But he can't just grab a candy bar from a vending machine or go for pizza or ice cream with friends after school. It's

Cooking with a friend can make learning to cook fun.

a real pain, and he's tired of it. Now that he's entering high school, his mom has decided Ernesto needs to take more control of his diet. She's teaching him more about food labels so he'll understand why he has to be so careful. He thinks it's lame.

In the grocery store, Ernesto and his mom look at ingredient lists on various foods. He checks a frozen pizza. There at the end of the list, it states: "Contains wheat, milk, and soy." Great. He's allergic to soy—and to several other legumes. In another aisle, he looks at a mayonnaise jar that states, "Contains eggs. May contain traces of milk, anchovies, peanuts, wheat, and soy." He continues to find that a lot of foods have a possibility of containing soy—so he must avoid them. Even canned tuna contains soy! He's beginning to wonder how his mom was able to keep soy out of his food all these years.

"You know," his mom says, "cooking is really chemistry." She knows he loved the chemistry part of his science class last year. "You could start learning to cook. You could learn to make good, safe snacks—and invite your friends home after school to try them."

Ernesto hadn't thought of that. It's not a bad idea, and maybe it could be fun—especially showing his friends that he can cook!

LIFE AFTER DIAGNOSIS

Once you are diagnosed with food allergies, perhaps the most painful idea you will have to absorb is that allergies have no cure. There is no magic pill or shot you can take to get rid of your food allergies. The only way to completely avoid allergy attacks is to completely avoid the foods to which you are allergic, even when there is only a possibility that you could eat a trace of the allergen. This is sometimes really frustrating, as Ernesto discovered, but it's not impossible and it won't ruin your life. Avoiding the food you're allergic to does require developing some new habits—and learning to pay close attention to what you eat.

As you navigate through this process, ask your parents for some help. Your doctor can also help and so can a registered dietitian, if one is available. So you're not in this alone. But, let's face it—as a teenager, you already spend a lot of time away from home, and soon you will be an adult. You owe it to yourself to become responsible for controlling your allergies as quickly as possible. You will

"There is no cure for food allergy. Strict avoidance is the only way to prevent a reaction, which can be caused by even small amounts of a food allergen."[1]

—"Living with Food Allergy," FAAN, 2010

feel better about yourself, and you will know how to stay safe.

Dealing with food allergies involves two basic steps. First, you must carefully avoid the foods you're allergic to, which means taking charge of your diet. Second, you must keep medications on hand at all times to counteract symptoms if allergic reactions occur.

TAKE CHARGE OF YOUR DIET

In the past, were you able to eat any food that sounded or looked good to you? Unfortunately, those days are over. From now on, everything you put in your mouth must be allergen-free. To make that happen, you must become a nutrition expert. You need to learn how to maintain a healthy, balanced diet while eliminating foods that negatively affect your immune system. You must also learn to read food labels, talk to food preparers, and find the information you need to separate your allergenic foods from your safe foods. The upside is that, with all this attention to your diet, you will likely become a very healthy person.

The key to avoiding food allergens is to know exactly what you're eating. One excellent approach is to eat as much fresh food—such as fruits and vegetables—as possible. Fresh foods contain more nutrients and they are purer—that is, an apple is just an apple; it doesn't contain

> "Manufacturers change the ingredients of their products frequently, and such changes are not always evident by looking at the front of a package. Read the ingredient label every time you purchase a food, even a familiar food."[2]
>
> —*"Living with Food Allergy," FAAN, 2010*

mysterious additives. However, it's best to buy organic to avoid pesticide contamination. And, of course, avoid any fruits and vegetables on your allergy list.

Also, be aware of the dangers of cross-contamination. Don't eat foods prepared with pans, dishes, or utensils that were previously used to prepare an allergenic food. For example, if you're allergic to peanuts, don't spread jam with a knife that was first used to spread peanut butter. Cross-reactivity is another potential problem. If you are allergic to one food, such as salmon, steer clear of trying other members of the same allergenic family of foods—other finned fish, for example.

READ FOOD LABELS

Before you eat any packaged food, always check its label. By law, labels must list all ingredients in a product and, if it contains a common allergen (eggs, milk, fish, shellfish, peanuts, tree nuts, wheat, or soy), the label should state this clearly. Be very careful—foods that you assume are safe might not be. You

Reading food labels will become a vital part of your life.

need to recognize that, for example, peanuts lurk in protein supplements, eggs are in mayonnaise, and milk is used in many baked goods. To find these hidden ingredients, you should learn the words on food labels that replace simpler words. For example, hydrolyzed vegetable protein might include peanuts, and albumin is the allergenic protein in eggs.

BE PREPARED FOR ALLERGIC ATTACKS

There are two categories of medications to deal with allergy symptoms: over-the-counter (OTC) remedies, such as antihistamines to handle

DECODING FOOD LABELS

Near the Nutrition Facts portion of a food label is a section titled "Ingredients." By law, this must list, in descending order of amount, every ingredient in the package. At the end of the list, it will state any major allergen that is or might be present. For example, the list on a package of Bisquick ends with the phrase "Contains wheat ingredients."

minor symptoms, and prescription medications, to deal with serious or life-threatening symptoms. These types of medications are taken after the onset of an allergic reaction. There are no medications you can take to prevent a reaction.

The OTC medications include antihistamines such as Benadryl, which combats symptoms caused by histamine release. Antihistamines relieve symptoms such as hives, swelling, runny or stuffy nose, watery eyes, and even abdominal pain.

If your food allergies result in asthma attacks, your doctor will prescribe a bronchodilator. This is a chemical such as albuterol that dilates, or opens, your airways and relieves symptoms such as shortness of breath, wheezing, or difficulty breathing. A bronchodilator is often prescribed as a handheld inhaler so you can take the medication anywhere.

DEAL WITH EMERGENCIES

If your allergies are severe and you are likely to go into anaphylaxis if you ingested an allergen, your doctor will prescribe epinephrine, which is also called adrenaline. This life-saving chemical dilates airways, raises blood pressure, and generally reverses the effects of anaphylaxis. Because it must be given within a few minutes after the onset of anaphylaxis, you must carry it with you at all times. Usually, the medication is contained in a small, single-dose autoinjector. A severe attack may require more than one injection, so your doctor may instruct you to carry at least two epinephrine autoinjectors.

USING AN AUTOINJECTOR

The major brands of epinephrine autoinjectors are EpiPen, which is a single autoinjector, and Twinject, which is a double autoinjector. To become proficient at using them, have an expert demonstrate the procedure and then practice with a trainer injector. Here is the procedure:

1. Remove the cap and grasp the injector in your fist with the tip pointing down.
2. Remove the safety release.
3. Jab the injector into your outer thigh and through any clothing, if necessary. Hold for ten seconds to release the medication.
4. Check that the medication was delivered. If it was not delivered, repeat Step 3.
5. Massage the injection site for ten seconds.
6. Call 9-1-1.
7. Prepare a second dose in case it's needed.

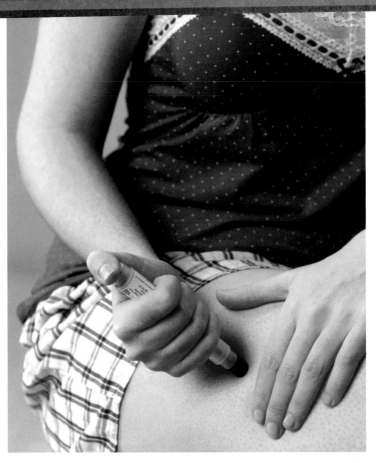

At some point you may need to use an epinephrine autoinjector. Be prepared for this emergency by having your medicine with you always.

If you do have an anaphylactic attack and receive an epinephrine injection, you should visit the emergency room immediately afterward. You may have a delayed reaction and require further treatment. Plus, you need to replace your used epinephrine autoinjector immediately. It is extremely important that you keep your epinephrine autoinjector with you at all times and that your family and close friends know how to use it. If you are unable to inject yourself, someone with you should be able to administer it. You may think that, if you are careful, you will never need to use the autoinjector, but you may ingest an unsafe food accidentally or you may have a reaction to a food you thought was safe. Always being prepared is your safest bet.

ASK YOURSELF THIS

- *How much do you know about eating a healthful diet while avoiding your food allergens? How can you learn more?*

- *What steps can you take to become more responsible for your diet?*

- *What are your medications for and how and when do you use them?*

- *Are you ever tempted to leave your medications at home when you go out? If so, why?*

- *What might happen if you leave your medications at home?*

6

I CAN DO THIS: COPING WITH FOOD ALLERGIES

Theresa just found out she is allergic to peanuts and tree nuts. So far, her symptoms have been fairly minor, but her doctor has cautioned her that this could change. The next reaction might be much more severe, even escalating to anaphylaxis. The worst part

You may be nervous to tell your friends about your food allergy, but if they are your true friends, they'll listen and be supportive.

for Theresa is telling her friends what's going on. They know she's been going to the doctor and has avoided going out to eat with them, but so far she hasn't told them why. She's nervous they're going to think she's a freak, and school is already hard enough as it is.

She has finally worked up her courage and goes with several friends to the ice cream shop after school. But she brings her own snack—an apple—and orders only a soft drink in a can. Even a plain vanilla cone might have been contaminated by nuts. When Shanice asks her, "What's going on with you lately?" Theresa takes a deep breath and says, "I have a food allergy."

Her friends look at each other and breathe a collective sigh of relief. "We thought it was something really awful," Shanice says. "So, what exactly is a food allergy?"

ENLIST FRIENDS AND FAMILY

It's one thing to deal with your allergy at home surrounded by your family and where you can control what you eat, but what happens when you're out in the world? If you're like Theresa, you might be embarrassed to tell your friends you have a food allergy. But, as Theresa found

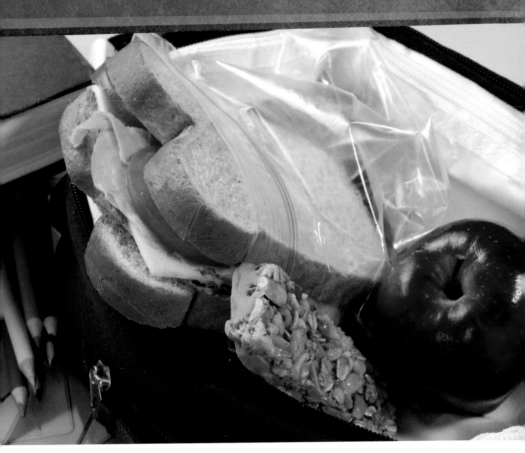

Bringing your own lunch ensures no cross-contamination with your food.

popcorn she made at home. When she goes to the mall, she packs her own lunch and eats in the food court with her friends. "In most cases," she says, "they end up being jealous that I have a home cooked meal while they're eating unappetizing junk food."[2]

That's okay most of the time, but what about dates? First, be open and honest about your food allergy. Make sure your date knows your allergies and understands the consequences if you eat the wrong thing. If you're dating someone with the same food allergy, you can avoid problems by ordering the same food your date orders. And yes, you can kiss! Just be sure your date has brushed his or her teeth and hasn't eaten any allergenic foods for several hours before.

AVOID ACCIDENTAL CONTACT

To avoid accidental contact with foods containing allergens, be alert for unlikely ways you may be exposed, such as:

- Picnics or buffets
- Skin contact
- Inhalation (from frying fish, boiling milk, or peanut dust)
- Dishes, utensils, or work surfaces used for more than one food
- Medications or cosmetics

BULLIES

Most people will accept your allergies and be friendly and supportive. But there's always the chance a bully or a jerk is in the crowd. How do you react when someone makes fun of you because of your food allergies? If it's a one-time thing, it's probably best to either laugh it off or ignore the person. But never put up with a persistent bully and *never* let anyone endanger you—for example, by trying to contaminate your food or daring you to eat something that will cause an allergic reaction. Colin, a 17-year-old with a peanut allergy, was shocked after someone smeared peanut butter on his school locker. He said,

One of the worst thoughts you could have when you are allergic to a type of food is that someone out there might risk your life for a joke. . . . I just want to let those kids that are going through similar situations know that they are not alone and are much stronger than they think. I would encourage anyone having a bad experience to reach out for help.[3]

If you need help handling a bullying situation, talk to a trusted adult.

RESTAURANTS

It may be intimidating at first, but if you have food allergies and you eat out, you must learn to talk to servers and food preparers about your condition. Whenever possible, ask to talk to the chef. Be matter-of-fact and courteous. Explain your food allergy and ask that they use special care when preparing your food to ensure that not only ingredients but also utensils and prep surfaces are free from allergens. Explain

MEDICAL ALERT BRACELET

A medical alert bracelet listing your allergies and emergency contact numbers will help medical responders diagnose your condition if you can't tell them. Make sure your friends know about your bracelet. Also, you could create a card that lists your allergies and emergency procedures to follow and keep it in your purse or backpack.

When ordering at a restaurant, make sure the server fully understands the severity of your food allergy.

the seriousness of your condition. An option is to download the "Chef Card" template from the FAAN Web site and fill it out, describing your specific needs. Keep copies with you, so you can give one to the server or chef.

TRAVELING

Traveling can be a challenge, but it's really not much different from any situation outside your home. Advance planning is the key. For a longer trip, make a detailed plan several weeks in advance. Include all aspects of your trip: from transportation to lodging and restaurants.

Discuss your allergies with the airline, and carry your own snacks plus alcohol wipes to clean surfaces. Stock up on your prescriptions before you leave and take plenty of Chef Cards for restaurants. You should also research medical facilities, just in case there is an emergency.

Ask your doctor to write a letter to show insurance companies, airlines, and others who might have questions or cause problems. For short trips, pack enough safe food for the whole trip. For longer trips, pack what you can and shop carefully at your destination, just as you do at home. The first few trips may be a little stressful because the process is new. But soon, your travel plan will become second nature, just like the other changes in your life.

"One of my main rules of eating out is, if you don't know what is in the food and someone can't tell you, don't eat it. It doesn't matter how much you would have liked to eat that dish; if you don't know what is in it, you would be risking your life. One has to be very careful when eating out at a restaurant!"[4]

—*Margot, age 14, allergic to peanuts and tree nuts*

ASK YOURSELF THIS

- *What specific things should you tell friends about your allergy?*

- *What is your written action plan for allergy emergencies? Do your friends and family have copies?*

- *What worries you most about dealing with your allergies in social situations? How can you prepare for these situations?*

- *How can you remain a normal teenager while still dealing responsibly with your food allergies?*

- *Who can you talk with about your concerns?*

BEING VIGILANT: LIFESTYLE CHANGES

Hakeem is running late. Track practice is in 45 minutes and he's starving! He has an exercise-induced food allergy, a specific kind of food allergy. Basically, if he eats certain foods within a certain period of exercising, he may have an allergic response and even go into anaphylaxis. His doctor has warned him not to eat anything—just to be on the safe side—at least three hours before exercising. But he's cheated once or twice before and nothing happened. He thinks the doctor is being overly cautious. *Surely, it can't hurt to have a quick snack*, he thinks. He throws together a peanut butter and jelly sandwich, gobbles it down, and rushes out the door.

At practice, Hakeem is soon winded and sweaty from jogging laps. On the fourth lap, he starts to feel hot and prickly, but he doesn't worry too much about it—after all, it's a really hot day. But on the fifth lap, he begins wheezing and has trouble catching his breath. He knows he's in trouble and veers off the track toward the coach. Coach Madison takes one look at his hive-covered face and says, "You're having an allergy attack." Fortunately, Hakeem and his parents have briefed the coach on Hakeem's allergies, and the coach runs for the first-aid kit. In it are Hakeem's medications, including an inhaler.

Several minutes after using the inhaler, Hakeem is breathing easier. Coach Madison gives him a dose of antihistamines to help with the hives and then calls Hakeem's mother. Hakeem can't figure out what happened.

Why did he have a reaction when he didn't
even eat soy? His mother reminds him that
people with soy allergies can sometimes react
to peanuts—especially when they exercise
too quickly after eating. Fortunately, Hakeem
avoided an anaphylactic reaction this time, but
the asthma attack scared him. He hadn't had
one for a while. He goes home early from track
practice, after promising both his mother and his
coach that he will never eat right before track
practice again.

MAKING CHANGES

Your new diet will be the most important
change in your life as you learn to live with
food allergies. But, as Hakeem found out, other
areas—including your exercise habits—will
have to change, too. You will need to allergy-
proof your home, a process that will involve

STAYING SAFE AT HOME
How do you stay safe at home? Follow these steps:
- Educate all family members and set up protective rules.
- Label and separate potentially allergenic foods.
- Stock up on safe foods and store them in a separate place.
- Find and use substitutes for allergenic foods.
- Eliminate the risk of cross-contamination.
- Avoid airborne allergens, such as open pots, steaming foods, and flour dust.
- Scrub and wash all food surfaces and utensils with soap and water.

your whole family. And you may need to study various alternative therapies or home remedies to determine if they work for you.

HOME CHANGES

When allergy-proofing your home, you and your family must strike a balance between keeping you safe, fulfilling the needs of other family

AVOIDING OTHER ALLERGY TRIGGERS

Proteins from nonfood sources or food additives may cause allergic reactions, although these are rare. Some examples include:

- Sulfite preservatives (used in cooked and processed foods)
- Benzoate and paraben preservatives (used in cosmetic products, food, and drugs)
- Aspirin (found in different medications)

members, and avoiding an irrational fear of the allergen. Suppose you are allergic to peanuts, but other family members love peanuts and peanut butter. Is the solution to ban peanuts from the house entirely or to keep them, but ensure they are eaten and prepared safely to reduce your exposure? Either solution can work. It's up to you and your family members to decide which will work best for the family.

For your safety, it is essential that your own food is not contaminated with peanuts (or any other allergen). This means keeping food surfaces clean, using clean containers and

Have separate containers in your home to store your nonallergenic food.

utensils, and not cross-contaminating any foods during cooking. And all family members should wash their hands frequently. But this does not mean you should have an irrational fear of the allergen. In fact, if the allergen is present in your home, you can become accustomed to living with it and be better prepared when you encounter it outside your home. Robert A. Wood, an allergist, said,

> *It's like having a gas stove or candles in your house. Children realize that the flame can harm*

them. They know not to touch the flame or play with fire, but when someone lights a match, they don't go running and screaming out of the house.[1]

An important part of living safely at home is educating family members and all others who spend time in your home, including babysitters, neighbors, and frequent guests. They should know the house rules about handling foods, and it's a good idea to post these rules on the refrigerator. You should keep an emergency kit containing medications on hand, and everyone should know how to find and use it. Having an information center that includes a list of actions to take in case of an emergency, emergency numbers, allergen-free recipes, and a reference book on food allergies is also helpful to have in the home.

EXERCISE

In general, exercise is a good thing. Every healthy person, with or without food allergies, should develop and maintain

COMMON FOOD SUBSTITUTES

- Instead of peanut butter, use soy butter.
- Instead of cow's milk, use rice, soy, oat, or potato milk.
- Instead of ice cream and yogurt, use milk-free ice cream and yogurt.
- Instead of butter, use oils, tahini, or sunflower butter.
- Instead of dairy cheese, use soy- or rice-based cheese, hummus, or tofu.

You can still exercise and be active like you used to be, but follow your doctor's advice on how long to wait after eating before you can begin.

a regular exercise program. Either team sports or individual sports such as running, walking, or swimming can improve your health if you exercise at least a half hour two to three days a week.

Someone with an exercised-induced food allergy must be especially careful, though. This allergic reaction is very rare and occurs in individuals who may not otherwise have a food allergy. But, exercise can trigger an allergic reaction when a person ingests a food within a few hours before doing strenuous exercise. Many foods are capable of triggering exercise-induced allergic reactions, including wheat, shellfish, peanuts, tomatoes, and corn. Often, the major symptoms are flushed skin and hives, but they can include wheezing and nausea. Sometimes the reaction can even escalate to anaphylaxis. So, don't stop exercising, but to be safe, take precautions. Don't eat for several hours before exercising, keep your epinephrine autoinjector and other medications handy, and exercise with a buddy.

ALTERNATIVE THERAPIES AND HOME REMEDIES

If you search the Internet looking for help with your food allergies, you may be bombarded with methods of diagnosis and "cures" that don't match what your doctor has told you. For example, a method called the ELISA/ACT tests claims to locate hidden or delayed allergies, which show symptoms from two hours to five days after ingestion instead of immediately. The patient's white blood cells are cultured and tested for reactions to as many as 300 substances, and treatment consists of dietary changes and supplements. However, these tests and others similar to it have not been scientifically validated.

"It is important to stress that self-help should only be an adjunct to proper medical treatment, never a substitute. Some allergic conditions can be life threatening; others can deteriorate to the point where they produce irreversible damage to health. No one should attempt to treat them without medical supervision."[2]

—*Jonathan Brostoff, MD, and Linda Gamlin, biochemist, counselor, writer, and expert on allergic diseases, 2000*

Many Web sites offer cures where none exist and hope you will believe their ideas by paying a lot of money for their tests, diagnoses, and ongoing treatments. Many of the people behind these ideas lack credentials as doctors, registered dietitians, or allergy specialists. Some people, although well-meaning, are promoting unscientific or unproven claims. And tests or treatments that require you to ingest or inject allergens may even be dangerous, as they may trigger an allergic attack. Such procedures should always be done under controlled conditions in a doctor's office.

If you really wish there were a cure for your condition, some of these claims might tempt you. Your doctor will probably tell you in no uncertain terms to avoid these online treatments, though, and use only the treatments he or she prescribes. Some vitamins or herbal remedies may help, and techniques such as yoga or meditation may benefit your overall health, even if they don't cure your allergies. Your best bet is to continue reading and learning. If you find a reasonable-sounding treatment you would like to try, discuss the idea with your parents and doctor. Together, you can make an informed decision.

ASK YOURSELF THIS

- *What can you do to make your home safe while keeping in mind the needs of other family members?*

- *Would you feel more comfortable removing food allergens from your home or keeping them, but carefully controlling them? Why?*

- *How can you incorporate healthy exercise into your life while avoiding exercise-related allergy attacks?*

- *Are you tempted by any alternative allergy treatments? If so, what ones? If such a treatment interests you, how can you verify claims about its safety and effectiveness?*

I CAN'T DO THIS: GETTING HELP

José has been feeling down lately. He's had wheat and soy allergies his whole life and it's always been a pain, but recently things seem to be getting worse. Not that the allergies are getting worse, but he's in high school now, and his allergies seem to get in the way of

Having a food allergy can be overwhelming. If you start feeling this way, ask for help.

everything he wants to do. He can't go out and eat pizza with his friends, because pizza crust contains wheat. He can't even grab a snack at a football game; he has to take his own. And now, Melissa wants him to take her out to dinner. He just wants to have a normal date, but he's going to have to tell her about his food allergies and then talk to the server. It can sometimes be so embarrassing and frustrating. If only there were someone to talk to—how do other kids handle this stuff?

José's mother notices him moping around and asks what's wrong. When José confesses his fears, his mother says, "You know, I think it's time you joined a support group. You need to talk to other kids your age about your allergies."

"Sounds great," José says glumly, "but it's not likely to happen. My friends are great, but none of them have food

"There's no question that living with a food allergy can be stressful—not only for the person with the allergy, but for the entire family. Don't hesitate to seek support or counseling if you or someone you love is experiencing feelings of depression, isolation, or fearfulness. Seeking help from a trusted clergyman, psychologist, or friend can get you through the tough times."[1]

—*The Food Allergy Initiative, 2011*

Talking with a trusted friend can help you feel better and release pent-up emotions.

allergies. They just don't understand what it's like."

"No, they don't," his mother agrees. "But just because we live in a small town doesn't mean we're cut off from the world. Let me show you something."

José's mother gets on the computer and pulls up a food allergy Web site. She shows José the teen section and suggests that he explore it. José is amazed. Kids his age are sharing stories about their allergies and describing how they handle different situations. There's a place to ask questions and get advice from someone who's gone through the same thing. José posts his fears about his first date with Melissa on the site's chat board and an hour later he has three great responses! A weight lifts from his shoulders. He is no longer alone with his food allergies.

FRIENDS AND FAMILY

It's important to realize, as José did, that you're not the only food allergy sufferer. Many people live with food allergies. If they can handle it, so can you! But where do you go for help? You've already learned it's important to enlist the help and cooperation of friends and family. Keep them updated on your situation. If something changes—if you get a new medication or are diagnosed with a new allergy—let them know. As you and your personal support group get used to dealing with food allergies, the process becomes easier. You will still remain aware of your allergies—in fact, it's important

CELEBRITIES WITH FOOD ALLERGIES

- Clay Aiken, singer: tree nuts, mushrooms, shellfish, coffee, chocolate, mint
- Drew Barrymore, actress: garlic, coffee
- Halle Berry, actress: shrimp
- Drew Brees, NFL quarterback: dairy, wheat, gluten, eggs, nuts
- Billy Bob Thornton, actor: wheat, shellfish, dairy products
- Serena Williams, professional tennis player: peanuts

BE A PAL

The Be a Pal: Protect a Life program from FAAN teaches kids five steps to keep friends with food allergies safe:

1. Take food allergies seriously—they're not a joke.
2. If a friend has food allergies, don't share food.
3. Always wash your hands after eating.
4. Help friends avoid their allergy foods.
5. Get help immediately if a friend has an allergic reaction.

that you do—but soon you and your friends and family will just accept them as a normal part of your life.

Food allergies are a lifelong health concern and outside sources of support are important. You should first turn to the medical personnel you already know— the doctor who diagnosed your allergies; the health practitioners who provided your first, most basic information on allergies; and possibly a dietician who helped you set up an allergen-free diet. You should always feel free to ask them questions or get references of other sources of help from them.

SUPPORT GROUPS

Maybe few or none of the people in your life have food allergies. Like José's friends, they're sympathetic, but they don't really understand what living with food allergies is like. Wouldn't it be nice to connect with other teens going

If you don't have a support group in your area, you can join one online.

through the same thing? That's what support groups are for. Talking to others with food allergies, asking them questions, listening to their experiences and insights—these can all be wonderful sources of emotional support. As you become more comfortable dealing with your own allergies, you can even begin providing support to others. Your doctor should be able to recommend a local support group, if one exists in your area.

Attending support group meetings and becoming friends with others near you who have food allergies can go a long way toward

> "Learn to advocate for yourself and ask questions. This will not only protect you and help you manage your allergy, but developing this skill will also help you with school and in many other aspects of life."[2]
>
> —*Brian, age 18, allergic to peanuts and tree nuts*

helping you deal with your allergies. But sometimes, there is no group nearby. Even if you do have local support, you can always check out online support groups. For food allergies, an excellent resource is FAAN. Its Web site contains a wealth of information and has a special section for teens that includes a Teen Advisory Group (TAG). TAG members write online articles and answer teens' questions about allergies. You can be as active in the group as you wish. You can read articles on the Web site, submit a specific question, or share your own experiences in an article or as a TAG member.

KEEP LEARNING

The more you know about your allergies, the less you will fear them and the more you can control them. Asking questions, joining a support group, and reading Web sites are all good ways to find information. Also, visit the library for books and magazine articles on food allergies, especially your specific allergies. Read everything you can find, but make sure the information is current. Allergy information changes quickly, because doctors and scientists are constantly collecting data and researching new treatment methods.

ASK YOURSELF THIS

- *What do you feel your friends don't understand about situations related to your food allergy?*

- *What problems have you wished you could discuss with someone who also has food allergies?*

- *Do you think a support group, either in person or online, would help you better cope with your allergies? If so, how?*

- *Do you feel you have any insights about living with food allergies that you could share with a group? If so, what are they?*

- *What sources of information do you currently use to learn about your allergies? What additional sources could you use?*

WHAT DOES THE
FUTURE HOLD?

Melanie has put up with food allergies for as long as she can remember. It's not fun. Lately, she has been discussing it with her best friend, Sasha. "Sometimes, I feel allergic to life!" she complains. "I can't imagine doing this forever."

While your friends may have good intentions, consult your medical team before making any choices that affect your allergy treatment.

Sasha is sympathetic. She thinks there must be a cure out there somewhere. There's so much information available; there must be something that will let Melanie eat all the food she's been missing out on. The girls decide they'll search the Internet. One Saturday morning, they sit in Melanie's bedroom glued to their laptops. Melanie searches "food allergy prevention" and Sasha types in "food allergy cures." Both get thousands of hits. This could take a while!

Melanie is already familiar with many of the medical sites with the same old information. She quickly dampens Sasha's enthusiasm about a claim that involves slowly introducing a food. "No, they're talking about food intolerance. That's different." But Sasha is getting more and more excited. "There are all kinds of sites talking about cures!" she insists. "I can't believe you don't know about these!" She reads off several claims. One says food allergies are psychological and can be cured by conditioning you to believe there's nothing wrong with the food. Another site lumps food allergies with food cravings, arthritis, and fatigue—and claims to cure them all!

Melanie shakes her head. "No, my doctor says those claims are not true. That stuff won't work, and some of it's dangerous."

"Yeah, well, your doctor's not coming up with anything new, is she?" Sasha asks. "Maybe she doesn't know about these new treatments. Things probably get on the Internet a lot faster than into those medical books she reads."

Melanie is tempted, but she knows the claims are probably not true. Also, she remembers her doctor saying some new cures and treatments are being tested. Maybe it's better to wait and stay safe.

LOOKING AHEAD

Like Melanie, you will have to deal with food allergies throughout your life. Sometimes it's depressing to think you will have to watch every bite of food you ever eat. But, although it seems slow, medical breakthroughs happen all the time. So what does the future hold? Are cures on the horizon? Will new treatments be able to prevent your allergic reactions or make them easier to control?

Right now, there are no cures for food allergies. Your only options are to avoid them or deal with them when you have a reaction. But doctors and scientists agree that your options could be much better in the future, and several avenues of research are currently being pursued. In the United States, the Food and Drug Administration (FDA) must approve new drugs or treatments. It is a process that takes many years: from the development of a cure or treatment, to testing it thoroughly, and then getting the FDA's approval. Most studies have been done in the laboratory or on animals such as mice, but some human studies are currently underway. Sometime in your life, you might even be asked to participate in such a study. What are some of the areas scientists are researching and testing?

DESENSITIZATION IMMUNOTHERAPY

Many people ask about the possibility of treating food allergies with injections. This form of immunotherapy, a treatment that changes the tolerance of the immune system, is used to treat allergens such as pollen or mold. Tiny

DNA IMMUNIZATION

Instead of using proteins, some proposed allergy vaccines may use deoxyribonucleic acid (DNA), the molecular structure that contains genetic information. Once inside the body's white blood cells, the DNA would begin producing the allergic protein. This would trick the body into thinking the protein belongs there, rather than thinking it's a foreign invader, so no allergic reaction would occur. DNA vaccines have been successfully tested on mice, but not yet on people. However, similar techniques are being used successfully for diseases such as cystic fibrosis and sickle-cell disease.

Desensitization immunotherapy looks promising as a treatment for food allergies. But, it should always be done under a doctor's care.

amounts of the allergen are periodically injected into a person's body for months or years. This builds up a tolerance, desensitizing the immune system so it will not overreact to the allergen. This works well for many environmental allergens, but because food allergies often cause life-threatening reactions, it has not yet been an effective treatment.

In sublingual immunotherapy, tiny drops of the allergen are placed under the tongue for immediate absorption, so you don't have to wait for a reaction. This has worked well for environmental allergens and has possibilities for treating food allergens, because reactions tend to be minor, often entailing only an itchy mouth. It tends not to cause systemic, or whole body, reactions, so it is less dangerous and treatments can sometimes be done at home. A recent study with hazelnuts was highly successful and other studies are underway.

In a third form of desensitization immunotherapy, you actually eat tiny amounts of the food containing the allergen under a doctor's supervision. If you can tolerate the food, you are allowed to consume it at home in the same tiny dose for several days or weeks. The amount of the food is gradually increased as your body becomes desensitized. Tests on milk, egg, and peanut allergies have given hopeful results.

HOMOLOGOUS PROTEIN IMMUNOTHERAPY

Some allergenic substances have homologous, or similar, protein allergens. For example, peanuts and soybeans both belong to the legume family, so they have similar proteins. Egg and chicken proteins are also similar. If a person with a severe peanut allergy is sensitized to soybean proteins, will his or her peanut allergy be decreased? According to some recent studies, the answer is yes. Researchers are excited about prospects for safer allergy immunotherapies that use similar, but not identical, proteins.

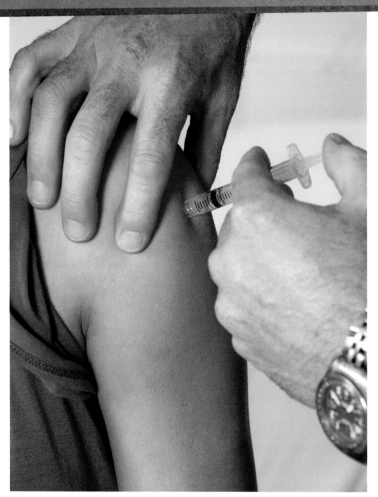

Someday vaccines may be used to prevent food allergies.

Although doctors have high hopes for desensitization immunotherapy, current reactions to the treatments are too unpredictable to be safe. So far, the sublingual approach appears to be the safest. Also, desensitization treatments are specific to a single allergen, so anyone with multiple allergies would require a separate treatment for each allergy.

MODIFIED PROTEIN VACCINES

Normally, the immune system produces antibodies to attack foreign invaders, such as bacteria or viruses. The antibodies help white blood cells fight the invaders. Disease vaccines contain killed or weakened strains of an invader, exposing you to enough of its protein antigen to trigger antibody production without triggering disease. Now, researchers are designing vaccines that have the opposite effect—they suppress or turn off the immune response. When an allergen enters the body, the immune system does not respond, so no allergic reaction occurs. As of 2011, these modified protein vaccines were not yet ready to test on people.

ANTI-IGE ANTIBODIES

Another treatment tries to outsmart the immune system by producing antibodies that work against the IgE antibodies that cause allergic reactions. The anti-IgE antibody would block histamine release by the immune system's IgE antibodies. A major

HOW ANTI-IGE ANTIBODIES WORK

Anti-IgEs are proteins specifically bioengineered to bind to the immune system's IgE antibodies. This prevents the IgEs from binding to mast cells and basophils. The mast cells and basophils then cannot release their histamines and no allergic reaction occurs.

benefit of this therapy is that it is not specific—it should work against any type of allergen, including food allergens, because they all cause the same IgE reaction.

Anti-IgE therapy has been successfully tested on hay fever symptoms and asthma, and one drug has been approved for use. Tests using this drug to treat peanut allergies are underway, but it will be several more years before testing is completed. When it works, this treatment does not cure allergies; it merely suppresses allergic reactions. If the person's blood IgE levels are very high, the treatment is ineffective. Also, it must be given regularly, probably every two to four weeks, to maintain protection, and the shots could be very expensive.

A FUTURE CURE?

Overall, prospects for new allergy treatments, and perhaps even a cure, look bright. Great progress will likely be made during your lifetime, although it may occur more slowly than you would like. Stay updated on the latest advances by reading magazine and journal articles and food allergy Web sites and by being active in local and online support groups. Discuss promising new treatments with your doctor and other experts. In short, get all the facts and decide how to use them. The best way to manage your food allergies is to take charge of your life and take an active role in your treatment.

ASK YOURSELF THIS

- *Have you asked your doctor about potential new treatments? Where did you learn about them? What did your doctor say?*

- *How would you feel about participating in a study on a new allergy treatment? What would be the pros and cons of such participation?*

- *Which of the potential treatments you have learned about seems most promising? Why?*

- *How do you see your life ten years from now? What part will your allergies play in your life?*

"Discovery of a treatment that can prevent food allergy or shut it down promises to be a long, slow process, but in the end, I am confident that eventually we will be able to treat food allergy such that the risk of anaphylactic reactions will be dramatically reduced or even eliminated.

In the long, long run—maybe 15 or 20 years down the road—I'm confident that we will be talking about curing food allergy, not just reducing reactions or their severity."[1]

—Robert A. Wood, MD, Chief of Pediatric Allergy and Immunology, Johns Hopkins University School of Medicine, 2007

JUST THE FACTS

Food allergies are an overreaction of the immune system to a food protein, a typically harmless substance. Food allergies cause histamine release and the formation of antibodies that act against the food allergen.

Approximately 12 million people in the United States, including 3 million children, have food allergies.

The highest incidence of food allergies is in children under age three; many allergies are outgrown by age five or six, while a few, including those to peanuts and seafood, may not appear until teen or adult years.

Only eight foods—cow's milk, eggs, peanuts, tree nuts, fish, shellfish, wheat, and soy—cause 90 percent of food allergies.

The most common food allergies in teens and adults are fish, shellfish, tree nuts, peanuts, and eggs.

Allergies are genetically based, but not all family members have allergies, and types of allergies may differ within a family.

People having one type of allergy may have or develop other allergies.

Non-life-threatening allergic reactions involve the skin and digestive system; they include some combination of flushed skin, hives, itching and swelling of the lips and tongue, runny or stuffy nose, and possibly nausea, vomiting, and abdominal pain.

Life-threatening reactions to food allergies involve the respiratory and circulatory systems and include asthma attacks and anaphylaxis.

Life-threatening reactions are most common after ingestion of peanuts or seafood, but they can occur after eating any of your allergenic foods.

Teens and young adults have the highest risk for life-threatening food allergy reactions because they tend to engage in riskier behaviors than the general population.

Typical allergy tests include skin prick tests and serum IgE tests.

There is no cure for food allergies, and the only way to prevent a reaction is to completely avoid your allergenic foods.

To avoid consuming allergenic foods, you must read food labels, talk to food preparers, and learn to prepare allergen-free foods.

Even if you have never had an anaphylactic reaction to a food, *always* be prepared for one: carry an epinephrine autoinjector plus prescription medications and antihistamines.

WHERE TO TURN

If You Feel Isolated Because of Your Food Allergy

A lot of socializing involves food, so it's easy to think you will never fit in because of your food allergies. But that's not true. Tell your close friends about your allergy. They will probably be very supportive. Although your friends may listen and try to help, they might not completely understand what you're going through, and you can still feel isolated. If this happens, look for local or online support groups to join. You can meet others your age who have similar circumstances. You can also exchange tips on how to cope with life as a teenager with a food allergy. Helping others can be rewarding for you, too. A great site to check out is FAAN's teen site, www.faanteen.org.

To Avoid Risks and Live Comfortably with Your Food Allergy

Living comfortably with your allergy is all about taking charge of your life and developing new, safe habits. With your family's cooperation, allergy-proof your home. Learn to prepare allergen-free food—both snacks and main dishes. Teach your family and friends about your allergies. Anticipate situations away from home where your allergies might be an issue and plan for them—not just school, but also social occasions, dates, vacations, and other activities. You must always watch your diet very carefully, and always carry your emergency kit with you. If you want to participate in an activity, first check it out with your parents and doctor, but with proper planning, you should be able to be involved with sports, music, or almost anything you want. Although you must be more vigilant and responsible than most teens, you can still live a normal, active teenage life, full of as much fun and adventure as you desire.

To Be Prepared for an Allergy Emergency

You hope you will never have an anaphylactic reaction, but you must always be prepared for one. This means always carrying your emergency medication with you. You should keep it on or very near you—in a purse, pocket, or backpack. You, your family, and close friends should know how to use the epinephrine autoinjector or other medication. If possible, wear a medical alert bracelet describing your allergies. Or, in your emergency kit, keep an allergy card that describes your allergies, lists emergency medical procedures (for example, give an epinephrine injection and call 9-1-1), and lists emergency contact numbers, including both your doctor and parents. Remember, if you go into anaphylactic shock, you must receive epinephrine within a few minutes, so you or someone nearby must give the injection. It can't wait until emergency medical technicians arrive.

If You Have a Friend with a Food Allergy

To support a friend who has food allergies, first understand that having a food allergy is a serious issue that can lead to harm or even death if not taken seriously. Learn all that you can. Ask your friend to describe his or her food allergies, symptoms, and how to handle emergencies. Understand that your friend can never eat the foods he or she is allergic to. Be alert to help ensure he or she never eats the wrong thing and to recognize a bad reaction if it happens. When you eat together, avoid contamination by washing your hands often and not touching his or her food or mixing it with your food. When your friend visits your home, make sure you have snacks that he or she can eat and prepare the food with separate containers and utensils. Most important, just be a friend. Be supportive and make sure he or she feels a part of the group.

GLOSSARY

allergic inflammatory response
Heat, redness, swelling, and pain initiated by the release of histamines and other chemicals.

antibody
A protein molecule made in response to the presence of an antigen that fights that antigen in an immune response; also called immunoglobulin.

antigen
A substance that is foreign to the body that initiates an immune response, including a disease or allergic reaction.

antihistamine
A chemical substance that blocks the action of histamine on tissues and thereby decreases allergy symptoms.

asthma
A chronic condition of the respiratory system in which inflammation, swelling, and closing of the airways makes breathing difficult.

epinephrine
A hormone produced by the adrenal gland and given to reverse symptoms of anaphylaxis; it opens airways and raises heart rate and blood pressure; also called adrenaline.

exercise-induced food allergy
A food allergy that is triggered by exercising shortly after food allergen consumption.

histamine
A chemical present in certain body cells that, when released, results in an allergic response.

immunotherapy
A form of treatment that changes the level of tolerance of the immune system; for example, it may restore the system's ability to fight disease or slowly condition it to accept an allergen.

mast cell
A type of white blood cell that lines the mouth and other parts of the digestive system.

ADDITIONAL RESOURCES

SELECTED BIBLIOGRAPHY

Brostoff, Jonathan, and Linda Gamlin. *Food Allergies and Food Intolerance*. Rochester, VT: Healing Arts Press, 2000. Print.

The Food Allergy & Anaphylaxis Network. The Food Allergy & Anaphylaxis Network, 2010. Web. 23 Jan. 2011.

"Food Allergy." *Mayo Clinic*. Mayo Foundation for Medical Education and Research, 2010. Web. 23 Jan. 2011.

Sicherer, Scott H. *Understanding and Managing Your Child's Food Allergies*. Baltimore, MD: Johns Hopkins UP, 2006. Print.

FURTHER READINGS

Bellenir, Karen, ed. *Allergy Information for Teens: Health Tips about Allergic Reactions such as Anaphylaxis, Respiratory Problems and Rashes*. Detroit, MI: Omnigraphics, 2006. Print.

Ehrlich, Paul M., and Elizabeth Shimer Bowers. *Living with Allergies*. New York: Facts on File, 2008. Print.

Joneja, Janice Vickerstaff. *Dealing with Food Allergies: A Practical Guide to Detecting Culprit Foods and Eating a Healthy, Enjoyable Diet*. Boulder, CO: Bull, 2003. Print.

WEB LINKS

To learn more about living with food allergies visit ABDO
Publishing Company online at **www.abdopublishing.com**.
Web sites about living with food allergies are featured on our
Book Links page. These links are routinely monitored and
updated to provide the most current information available.

SOURCE NOTES

CHAPTER 1. HOW CAN I BE ALLERGIC TO FOOD?

1. Scott H. Sicherer. "Food Allergies." *Medscape Reference*. WebMD, 14 Dec. 2010. Web. 22 Dec. 2010.

2. "Food Allergy Facts & Statistics." *The Food Allergy & Anaphylaxis Network*. The Food Allergy & Anaphylaxis Network, 2010. Web. 30 Dec. 2010.

3. Ibid.

CHAPTER 2. WHY ME? CAUSES

1. Scott H. Sicherer. *Understanding and Managing Your Child's Food Allergies*. Baltimore, MD: Johns Hopkins UP, 2006. Print. 64.

2. Ibid.

3. "Food Allergy Facts & Statistics." *The Food Allergy & Anaphylaxis Network*. The Food Allergy & Anaphylaxis Network, 2010. Web. 17 Nov. 2010.

4. "Allergy Statistics." *American Academy of Allergy Asthma & Immunology*. American Academy of Allergy Asthma & Immunology, 2010. Web. 30 Dec. 2010.

5. Ibid.

6. Ibid.

7. Rhonda Merritt. "Fish & Shellfish Allergies." *eHow Health*. Demand Media, Inc. 18 May 2010. Web. 31 Dec. 2010.

8. Charlene Laino. "Sesame Allergies on the Rise in U.S." *WebMD*. WebMD, 16 Mar. 2009. Web. 31 Dec. 2010.

9. Ibid.

10. Rhonda Merritt. "Fish & Shellfish Allergies." *eHow Health*. Demand Media, Inc. 18 May 2010. Web. 31 Dec. 2010.

CHAPTER 3. JUST ONE BITE:
RISK FACTORS AND COMPLICATIONS

1. Scott H. Sicherer. *Understanding and Managing Your Child's Food Allergies*. Baltimore, MD: Johns Hopkins UP, 2006. Print. 253.

2. Darryl Zeldin. "Children, Males, and Blacks are at Increased Risk for Food Allergies." *National Institute of Environmental Health Sciences—National Institutes of Health*. Department of Health and Human Services. 4 Oct. 2010. Web. 1 Jan. 2011.

3. Robert A. Wood and Joe Kraynak. *Food Allergies for Dummies*. Indianapolis, IN: Wiley, 2007. Print. 249.

4. Darryl Zeldin. "Children, Males, and Blacks are at Increased Risk for Food Allergies." *National Institute of Environmental Health Sciences—National Institutes of Health*. Department of Health and Human Services. 4 Oct. 2010. Web. 1 Jan. 2011.

5. "Allergy Statistics." *American Academy of Allergy Asthma & Immunology*. American Academy of Allergy Asthma & Immunology, 2010. Web. 30 Dec. 2010.

6. Melissa Conrad Stöppler. "Food Allergy." *MedicineNet. com*. MedicineNet, 2010. Web. 17 Nov. 2010.

SOURCE NOTES CONTINUED

CHAPTER 4. DO I HAVE ONE?
TESTING AND DIAGNOSIS

1. "Allergy Statistics." *American Academy of Allergy Asthma & Immunology.* American Academy of Allergy Asthma & Immunology, 2010. Web. 30 Dec. 2010.

2. Robert A. Wood and Joe Kraynak. *Food Allergies for Dummies.* Indianapolis, IN: Wiley, 2007. Print. 85.

CHAPTER 5. EATING THE RIGHT FOODS: TREATMENT

1. "Living with Food Allergy." *The Food Allergy & Anaphylaxis Network.* The Food Allergy & Anaphylaxis Network, 2010. Web. 17 Nov. 2010.

2. Ibid.

CHAPTER 6. I CAN DO THIS: COPING WITH FOOD ALLERGIES

1. "Food Allergies Don't Stop Me." *The Food Allergy & Anaphylaxis Network.* The Food Allergy & Anaphylaxis Network, 4 Jan. 2011. Web. 7 Jan. 2011.

2. Ibid.

3. "A Bullying Victim's Perspective." *The Food Allergy & Anaphylaxis Network.* The Food Allergy & Anaphylaxis Network, 2006. Web. 7 Jan. 2011.

4. "Food Allergies in the Real World: Careful and Safe." *Food Allergies in the Real World.* The Food Allergy & Anaphylaxis Network, n.d. Web. 4 Jan. 2011.

CHAPTER 7. BEING VIGILANT: LIFESTYLE CHANGES

1. Robert A. Wood and Joe Kraynak. *Food Allergies for Dummies*. Hoboken, NJ: Wiley, 2007. Print. 171.
2. Jonathan Brostoff and Linda Gamlin. *Food Allergies and Food Intolerance*. Rochester, VT: Healing Arts, 2000. Print. 56.

CHAPTER 8. I CAN'T DO THIS: GETTING HELP

1. "Emotional Issues." *Food Allergy Initiative*. Food Allergy Initiative, n.d. Web. 26 May 2011.
2. "Back-to-School Tips." *Food Allergies in the Real World*. The Food Allergy & Anaphylaxis Network, 2010. Web. 22 Jan. 2011.

CHAPTER 9. WHAT DOES THE FUTURE HOLD?

1. Robert A. Wood and Joe Kraynak. *Food Allergies for Dummies*. Hoboken, NJ: Wiley, 2007. Print. 153.

INDEX

ABOUT THE AUTHOR

Carol Hand has a doctorate in zoology and has taught college biology, written middle and high school science curricula, and authored several young-adult science books. She works as a freelance writer of science books and online courses.

PHOTO CREDITS